☆1 Master Mix

51 Breads

Printed in the United States of America
by G&R Publishing Co.

Distributed By:

507 Industrial Street
Waverly, IA 50677

ISBN 1-56383-148-1
Item #3604

How to Use This Book

Begin by stirring up a batch of the Master Mix to store in your cupboard. When you find yourself craving homemade bread, just start with a few cups of your Master Mix, then add your wet ingredients and yummy extras. One Master Mix makes it a snap to bake up a loaf of fresh bread!

All of the bread recipes make 1 loaf.

Recipes shown on the front cover:

1

Master Mix for Breads

Makes enough for 6 to 8 bread recipes

12 1/2 C. flour
5 T. baking powder
1 T. baking soda
2 tsp. salt
3 1/2 C. sugar
2 C. brown sugar

2

Combine flour, baking powder, baking soda and salt together and mix thoroughly with a wire whisk, making sure to break up any flour lumps. Add sugar and brown sugar, making sure to break up any clumps in the brown sugar with your fingers. Once again, mix thoroughly until evenly combined.

Store mix in a tightly covered container in a cool, dry place.

Before using, be sure to give the mix a good stir as ingredients of different particle size may settle at different levels over time.

The Master Mix will keep for three to four months.

Gingerbread Loaf

1/3 C. vegetable oil
2 eggs
1/2 C. molasses
1 C. buttermilk
1 tsp. vanilla
1 1/2 tsp. ginger
1 tsp. cinnamon
1/2 tsp. cloves
3 C. Master Mix
1 1/2 C. raisins

4

Preheat oven to 350°.

In a large mixing bowl, mix the vegetable oil, eggs, molasses, buttermilk, vanilla, ginger, cinnamon and cloves until thoroughly combined.

Add Master Mix and stir until just combined. Fold raisins into the batter.

Pour batter into a greased loaf pan. Bake for 55 to 65 minutes or until a toothpick inserted into the center comes out clean.

Cappuccino Chocolate Chip Bread

1/2 C. margarine, melted
2 eggs
1 C. milk
1 tsp. vanilla
2 T. instant cappuccino mix
3 C. Master Mix
1 1/2 C. chocolate chips

Preheat oven to 350°.

In a large mixing bowl, mix the margarine, eggs, milk, vanilla and cappuccino mix until thoroughly combined.

Add Master Mix and stir until just combined. Fold chocolate chips into the batter.

Pour batter into a greased loaf pan. Bake for 45 to 55 minutes or until a toothpick inserted into the center comes out clean.

Marble Bread

1/2 C. margarine, melted
2 eggs
1 C. milk
1 tsp. vanilla
3 C. Master Mix
1/2 C. semi-sweet chocolate chips
2 T. margarine
1 T. water
1 T. baking cocoa

In a large mixing bowl, mix the margarine, eggs, milk and vanilla and stir until thoroughly combined.

Add Master Mix and stir until just combined.

In a separate bowl, combine chocolate chips, margarine, water and baking cocoa. Melt mixture in a double boiler. This can also be melted in the microwave, but must be done very carefully as chocolate can easily overheat. Once overheated, the chocolate becomes stiff (instead of a smooth liquid) and will not incorporate into the batter.

Preheat oven to 350°.

Transfer half of bread dough into a separate bowl and stir in the melted chocolate mixture until fully combined and evenly colored.

In a loaf pan, pour each batter along side the other so that they extend lengthwise down the pan. With a broad knife, use a folding motion (as one would to fold berries into a batter) to create a marbled or swirled effect in the batter. Bake for 45 to 55 minutes or until a toothpick inserted in the center comes out clean.

Tropical Bread

1/2 C. margarine, melted
2 eggs
1-11 oz. can mandarin oranges*
1/2 C. milk
1/2 C. orange juice
3 C. Master Mix
1 C. white chocolate chips
3/4 C. flaked coconut

*Drain the juice and coarsely chop the oranges into
halves or thirds with the side of a fork or a knife.

10

Preheat oven to 350°.

In a large mixing bowl, mix the margarine, eggs, mandarin oranges, milk and orange juice until thoroughly combined.

Add Master Mix and stir just until combined. Fold white chocolate chips and coconut into the batter.

Pour batter into a greased loaf pan. Bake for 55 to 65 minutes or until a toothpick inserted into the center comes out clean.

Raspberry Almond Bread

1/2 C. margarine, melted
2 eggs
1 C. milk
1 1/2 tsp. almond extract
3 C. Master Mix
3/4 C. sliced almonds
1 1/2 C. raspberries (fresh or frozen,
   thawed)

12

Preheat oven to 350°.

In a large mixing bowl, mix the margarine, eggs, milk and almond extract until thoroughly combined.

Add Master Mix and stir until just combined. Fold in almonds and raspberries using just a few quick turns as berries will bleed out juice if over mixed with the batter.

Pour batter into a greased loaf pan. Bake for 45 to 55 minutes or until a toothpick inserted into the center comes out clean.

Carrot Pineapple Bread

1/2 C. vegetable oil
2 eggs
1/2 C. sour cream
1-8 oz. can crushed pineapple including
   juice
3 C. Master Mix
1 1/2 C. shredded carrots
1/2 tsp. nutmeg

Preheat oven to 350°.

In a large mixing bowl, mix the vegetable oil, eggs, sour cream and crushed pineapple until thoroughly combined.

Add Master Mix and stir until just combined. Fold carrots and nutmeg into the batter.

Pour batter into a greased loaf pan. Bake for 55 to 65 minutes or until a toothpick inserted into the center comes out clean.

Chocolate Peanut Butter Chip Bread

1/2 C. margarine, melted
2 eggs
1 tsp. vanilla
3/4 C. baking cocoa
1 C. milk
2 1/2 C. Master Mix
1 1/2 C. peanut butter chips

16

Preheat oven to 350°.

In a large mixing bowl, mix the margarine, eggs, vanilla, cocoa and milk until thoroughly combined.

Add Master Mix and stir until just combined. Fold peanut butter chips into the batter.

Pour batter into a greased loaf pan. Bake for 45 to 55 minutes or until a toothpick inserted into the center comes out clean.

Sweet Potato Marshmallow Bread

1/2 C. vegetable oil
2 eggs
1 C. milk
1 C. sweet potatoes, pureed or well
    mashed
1 tsp. vanilla
1/2 tsp. nutmeg
3 C. Master Mix
1 1/2 C. miniature marshmallows

18

Preheat oven to 350°.

In a large mixing bowl, mix the vegetable oil, eggs, milk, sweet potatoes, vanilla and nutmeg until thoroughly combined.

Add Master Mix and stir until just combined. Fold miniature marshmallows into the batter.

Pour batter into a greased loaf pan. Bake for 55 to 65 minutes or until a toothpick inserted into the center comes out clean.

Chocolate Banana Bread

1/2 C. margarine, melted
2 eggs
1 tsp. vanilla
3/4 C. baking cocoa
1 C. milk
1 C. mashed bananas (about 3 bananas)
3 C. Master Mix

20

Preheat oven to 350°.

In a large mixing bowl, mix the margarine, eggs, vanilla, cocoa, milk and bananas until thoroughly combined.

Add Master Mix and stir until just combined.

Pour batter into a greased loaf pan. Bake for 55 to 65 minutes or until a toothpick inserted into the center comes out clean.

Orange
Poppy Seed Bread

1/2 C. vegetable oil
2 eggs
2/3 C. orange juice
1 tsp. orange extract
1/2 C. milk
2 tsp. orange zest
3 C. Master Mix
2 T. poppy seeds

22

Preheat oven to 350°.

In a large mixing bowl, mix the vegetable oil, eggs, orange juice, orange extract, milk and orange zest until thoroughly combined.

Add Master Mix and stir until just combined. Fold poppy seeds into the batter.

Pour batter into a greased loaf pan. Bake for 45 to 55 minutes or until a toothpick inserted into the center comes out clean.

Zucchini Bread

1/2 C. vegetable oil
2 eggs
1 C. buttermilk
1/2 tsp. nutmeg
1/2 tsp. cinnamon
1 1/2 C. grated zucchini
3 C. Master Mix
1 C. chopped pecans or walnuts

Preheat oven to 350°.

In a large mixing bowl, mix the vegetable oil, eggs, buttermilk, nutmeg, cinnamon and grated zucchini until thoroughly combined.

Add Master Mix and stir until just combined. Fold chopped pecans or walnuts into the batter.

Pour batter into a greased loaf pan. Bake for 55 to 65 minutes or until a toothpick inserted into the center comes out clean.

Strawberry
Sour Cream Bread

1/2 C. margarine, melted
2 eggs
1 tsp. vanilla
1 C. sour cream
1/3 C. milk
3 C. Master Mix
1 1/2 C. strawberries, chopped (fresh or
    frozen, thawed)

Preheat oven to 350°.

In a large mixing bowl, mix the margarine, eggs, vanilla, sour cream and milk until thoroughly combined.

Add Master Mix and stir until just combined. Fold in strawberries using just a few quick turns as berries will bleed out juice if over mixed with the batter.

Pour batter into a greased loaf pan. Bake for 55 to 65 minutes or until a toothpick inserted into the center comes out clean.

Banana Nut Bread

1/2 C. vegetable oil
2 eggs
1 tsp. vanilla
1/2 tsp. nutmeg
1 C. mashed bananas (about 3 bananas)
3/4 C. milk
3 C. Master Mix
1 C. chopped walnuts

Preheat oven to 350°.

In a large mixing bowl, mix the vegetable oil, eggs, vanilla, nutmeg, bananas and milk until thoroughly combined.

Add Master Mix and stir until just combined. Fold chopped walnuts into the batter.

Pour batter into a greased loaf pan. Bake for 55 to 65 minutes or until a toothpick inserted into the center comes out clean.

Carrot-Raisin & Spice Bread

1/2 C. vegetable oil
2 eggs
1/2 C. orange juice
1/2 C. crushed
   pineapple,
   well drained
2/3 C. raisins
1 C. shredded carrots

1/2 tsp. cinnamon
1/2 tsp. nutmeg
1/2 tsp. ginger

1/2 tsp. allspice
1/2 C. milk
3 C. Master Mix

Preheat oven to 350°.

In a large mixing bowl, mix the vegetable oil, eggs, orange juice, pineapple, raisins, carrots, cinnamon, nutmeg, ginger, allspice and milk until thoroughly combined.

Add Master Mix and stir until just combined.

Pour batter into a greased loaf pan. Bake for 55 to 65 minutes or until a toothpick inserted into the center comes out clean.

Apricot Bread

1/2 C. vegetable oil
2 eggs
1/2 C. apricot nectar
1/2 C. milk
3 C. Master Mix
1 C. chopped dried apricots

Preheat oven to 350°.

In a large mixing bowl, mix the vegetable oil, eggs, apricot nectar and milk until thoroughly combined.

Add Master Mix and stir until just combined. Fold dried apricots into the batter.

Pour batter into a greased loaf pan. Bake for 45 to 55 minutes or until a toothpick inserted into the center comes out clean.

Chocolate Cherry Bread

1/2 C. margarine, melted
2 eggs
1 tsp. vanilla
3/4 C. baking cocoa
1 C. milk
2 1/2 C. Master Mix
3/4 C. chopped pecans
1 1/2 C. chopped maraschino cherries

Preheat oven to 350°.

In a large mixing bowl, mix the margarine, eggs, vanilla, cocoa and milk until thoroughly combined.

Add Master Mix and stir until just combined. Fold in pecans and maraschino cherries using just a few quick turns as the cherries will bleed out juice if over mixed with the batter.

Pour batter into a greased loaf pan. Bake for 45 to 55 minutes or until a toothpick inserted into the center comes out clean.

Raisin Bran Bread

1/2 C. vegetable oil
1/2 C. molasses
2 eggs
1 C. milk
2 1/2 C. Master Mix
1 C. wheat bran
1 C. raisins

Preheat oven to 350°.

In a large mixing bowl, mix the vegetable oil, molasses, eggs and milk until thoroughly combined.

Add Master Mix and wheat bran until just combined. Fold raisins into the batter.

Pour batter into a greased loaf pan. Bake for 45 to 55 minutes or until a toothpick inserted into the center comes out clean.

Apricot-Pecan
& White Chip Bread

1/2 C. vegetable oil
2 eggs
1/2 C. orange juice
1/2 C. milk
3 C. Master Mix
3/4 C. chopped dried apricots
3/4 C. chopped pecans
1 C. white chocolate chips

Preheat oven to 350°.

In a large mixing bowl, mix the vegetable oil, eggs, orange juice and milk until thoroughly combined.

Add Master Mix and stir until just combined. Fold apricots, pecans and white chocolate chips into the batter.

Pour batter into a greased loaf pan. Bake for 45 to 55 minutes or until a toothpick inserted into the center comes out clean.

Pumpkin Pecan Bread

1/2 C. vegetable oil
2 eggs
1 C. milk
1 C. canned pumpkin
1 tsp. vanilla
1 tsp. cinnamon
1/2 tsp. nutmeg
1/2 tsp. ginger
1/2 tsp. allspice
3 C. Master Mix
3/4 C. chopped pecans

40

Preheat oven to 350°.

In a large mixing bowl, mix the vegetable oil, eggs, milk, pumpkin, vanilla, cinnamon, nutmeg, ginger and allspice until thoroughly combined.

Add Master Mix and stir until just combined. Fold pecans into the batter.

Pour batter into a greased loaf pan. Bake for 55 to 65 minutes or until a toothpick inserted into the center comes out clean.

Apple Cinnamon Nut Bread

1/2 C. margarine, melted
2 eggs
1 C. milk
1/2 tsp. nutmeg
1 1/2 tsp. cinnamon
1 1/2 C. shredded apples
3 C. Master Mix
1 C. chopped pecans

Preheat oven to 350°.

In a large mixing bowl, mix the margarine, eggs, milk, nutmeg, cinnamon and shredded apples until thoroughly combined.

Add Master Mix and stir until just combined. Fold pecans into the batter.

Pour batter into a greased loaf pan. Bake for 55 to 65 minutes or until a toothpick inserted into the center comes out clean.

Banana Coconut Bread

1/2 C. vegetable oil
2 eggs
1 C. milk
1 tsp. coconut extract or coconut
    flavoring
1 C. mashed bananas (about 3 bananas)
3 C. Master Mix
1 C. shredded or flaked coconut

Preheat oven to 350°.

In a large mixing bowl, mix the vegetable oil, eggs, milk, coconut extract and bananas until thoroughly combined.

Add Master Mix and stir until just combined. Fold coconut into the batter.

Pour batter into a greased loaf pan. Bake for 55 to 65 minutes or until a toothpick inserted into the center comes out clean.

Lemon Ginger Bread

1/2 C. vegetable oil
2 eggs
2 tsp. lemon zest
1 tsp. lemon extract
1 C. milk
2 tsp. ginger
3 C. Master Mix

Preheat oven to 350°.

In a large mixing bowl, mix the vegetable oil, eggs, lemon zest, lemon extract, milk and ginger until thoroughly combined.

Add Master Mix and stir until just combined.

Pour batter into a greased loaf pan. Bake for 45 to 55 minutes or until a toothpick inserted into the center comes out clean.

Maple Nut Loaf

1/2 C. margarine, melted
2 eggs
1/2 C. maple syrup (be sure to use real
    maple syrup, or one with a good strong
    maple flavor)
1 C. milk
3 C. Master Mix
3/4 C. chopped pecans or walnuts

Preheat oven to 350°.

In a large mixing bowl, mix the margarine, eggs, maple syrup and milk until thoroughly combined.

Add Master Mix and stir until just combined. Fold pecans or walnuts into the batter.

Pour batter into a greased loaf pan. Bake for 45 to 55 minutes or until a toothpick inserted into the center comes out clean.

Blueberry Oat Bread

1/2 C. margarine, melted
2 eggs
1 C. milk
1 tsp. vanilla
1/2 tsp. cinnamon
1/2 tsp. nutmeg
2 1/4 C. Master Mix
1 C. oatmeal
1 C. blueberries (fresh or frozen,
    thawed)

50

Preheat oven to 350°.

In a large mixing bowl, mix the margarine, eggs, milk, vanilla, cinnamon and nutmeg until thoroughly combined.

Add Master Mix and oatmeal and stir until just combined. Fold in blueberries using just a few quick turns as berries will bleed out juice if over mixed with the batter.

Pour batter into a greased loaf pan. Bake for 45 to 55 minutes or until a toothpick inserted into the center comes out clean.

Peanut Butter &
Milk Chocolate Bread

1/2 C. margarine, melted
1/2 C. peanut butter
2 eggs
1 tsp. vanilla
1 C. milk
3 C. Master Mix
1 1/2 C. milk chocolate chips or coarsely
    chopped milk chocolate bars

52

Preheat oven to 350°.

In a large mixing bowl, mix the margarine, peanut butter, eggs, vanilla and milk until thoroughly combined.

Add Master Mix and stir until just combined. Fold chocolate chips into the batter.

Pour batter into a greased loaf pan. Bake for 45 to 55 minutes or until a toothpick inserted into the center comes out clean.

Cranberry Apple Bread

1/2 C. vegetable oil
2 eggs
1/2 C. apple cider
1/2 C. milk
1 C. shredded apples
3 C. Master Mix
3/4 C. chopped walnuts or pecans
1 C. chopped cranberries (fresh or
    frozen, thawed)

Preheat oven to 350°.

In a large mixing bowl, mix the vegetable oil, eggs, apple cider, milk and shredded apples until thoroughly combined.

Add Master Mix and stir until just combined. Fold in walnuts or pecans and cranberries using just a few quick turns as berries will bleed out juice if over mixed with the batter.

Pour batter into a greased loaf pan. Bake for 55 to 65 minutes or until a toothpick inserted into the center comes out clean.

Zucchini Date Chocolate Chip Bread

1/2 C. margarine, melted
2 eggs
1 C. shredded zucchini
1 tsp. vanilla
1 C. milk
3 C. Master Mix
1 C. chopped dates
1 C. chocolate chips
1/2 C. chopped walnuts or pecans

56

Preheat oven to 350°.

In a large mixing bowl, mix the margarine, eggs, zucchini, vanilla and milk until thoroughly combined.

Add Master Mix and stir until just combined. Fold dates, chocolate chips and walnuts or pecans into the batter.

Pour batter into a greased loaf pan. Bake for 55 to 65 minutes or until a toothpick inserted into the center comes out clean.

Nectarine Yogurt Bread

1/2 C. vegetable oil
2 eggs
1 1/3 C. vanilla flavored yogurt
3 C. Master Mix
1 1/2 C. chopped fresh nectarines

58

Preheat oven to 350°.

In a large mixing bowl, mix the vegetable oil, eggs and vanilla flavored yogurt until thoroughly combined.

Add Master Mix and stir until just combined. Fold nectarines into the batter.

Pour batter into a greased loaf pan. Bake for 55 to 65 minutes or until a toothpick inserted into the center comes out clean.

Cheesy Apple & White Chocolate Bread

1/2 C. margarine, melted
2 eggs
1 tsp. vanilla
1 C. milk
1 C. shredded apples
3 C. Master Mix
1 C. shredded Jack cheese
1 C. white chocolate chips

60

Preheat oven to 350°.

In a large mixing bowl, mix the margarine, eggs, vanilla, milk and shredded apples until thoroughly combined.

Add Master Mix and stir until just combined. Fold cheese and white chocolate chips into the batter.

Pour batter into a greased loaf pan. Bake for 55 to 65 minutes or until a toothpick inserted into the center comes out clean.

Peach Pecan Bread

1/2 C. margarine, melted
2 eggs
1 C. buttermilk
1 tsp. vanilla
3 C. Master Mix
1 C. chopped pecans
1 1/2 C. chopped peaches (fresh, canned
   or frozen, thawed)

Preheat oven to 350°.

In a large mixing bowl, mix the margarine, eggs, buttermilk and vanilla until thoroughly combined.

Add Master Mix and stir until just combined. Fold pecans and peaches into the batter.

Pour batter into a greased loaf pan. Bake for 55 to 65 minutes or until a toothpick inserted into the center comes out clean.

Honey-Nut Oatmeal Loaf

1/2 C. margarine, melted
2 eggs
1/2 C. honey
1 C. buttermilk
2 1/2 C. Master Mix
1 C. oatmeal
1/2 C. chopped pecans

Preheat oven to 350°.

In a large mixing bowl, mix the margarine, eggs, honey and buttermilk until thoroughly combined.

Add Master Mix and oatmeal and stir until just combined. Fold pecans into the batter.

Pour batter into a greased loaf pan. Bake for 55 to 65 minutes or until a toothpick inserted into the center comes out clean.

Orange Apple Bread

1/2 C. vegetable oil
2 eggs
1/2 C. orange juice
2 tsp. orange zest
1/2 C. milk
1 1/2 C. grated apples
3 C. Master Mix

Preheat oven to 350°.

In a large mixing bowl, mix the vegetable oil, eggs, orange juice, orange zest, milk and grated apples until thoroughly combined.

Add Master Mix and stir until just combined.

Pour batter into a greased loaf pan. Bake for 55 to 65 minutes or until a toothpick inserted into the center comes out clean.

Pumpkin Chocolate Chip Bread

1/2 C. vegetable oil
2 eggs
1 tsp. cinnamon
1/2 tsp. nutmeg
1 C. canned pumpkin
1 C. milk
3 C. Master Mix
1 C. chocolate chips

68

Preheat oven to 350°.

In a large mixing bowl, mix the vegetable oil, eggs, cinnamon, nutmeg, pumpkin and milk until thoroughly combined.

Add Master Mix and stir until just combined. Fold chocolate chips into the batter.

Pour batter into a greased loaf pan. Bake for 55 to 65 minutes or until a toothpick inserted into the center comes out clean.

Cherry Oat Bread

1/2 C. margarine, melted
2 eggs
1 C. buttermilk
2 1/4 C. Master Mix
1 C. oatmeal
1 C. dried tart cherries

Preheat oven to 350°.

In a large mixing bowl, mix the margarine, eggs and buttermilk until thoroughly combined.

Add Master Mix and oatmeal and stir until just combined. Fold cherries into the batter.

Pour batter into a greased loaf pan. Bake for 45 to 55 minutes or until a toothpick inserted into the center comes out clean.

Rhubarb Bread

1/2 C. butter
1 1/2 C. chopped rhubarb
2 eggs
1 C. milk
3 C. Master Mix

Sauté rhubarb in butter. Allow to cool slightly before adding to the rest of ingredients.

Preheat oven to 350°.

In a large mixing bowl, mix the sautéed rhubarb, eggs and milk until thoroughly combined.

Add Master Mix and stir until just combined.

Pour batter into a greased loaf pan. Bake for 55 to 65 minutes or until a toothpick inserted into the center comes out clean.

mon Craisin Loaf

1/2 C. vegetable oil
2 eggs
1/4 C. lemon juice
2 tsp. lemon zest
3/4 C. milk
3 C. Master Mix
1 C. craisins

74

Preheat oven to 350°.

In a large mixing bowl, mix the vegetable oil, eggs, lemon juice, lemon zest and milk until thoroughly combined.

Add Master Mix and stir until just combined. Fold craisins into the batter.

Pour batter into a greased loaf pan. Bake for 45 to 55 minutes or until a toothpick inserted into the center comes out clean.

Cranberry Orange Bread

1/2 C. vegetable oil
2 eggs
1 tsp. orange extract
1 T. orange zest
1 C. milk
3 C. Master Mix
1 C. chopped cranberries (fresh or
  frozen, thawed)

Preheat oven to 350°.

In a large mixing bowl, mix the vegetable oil, eggs, orange extract, orange zest and milk until thoroughly combined.

Add Master Mix and stir until just combined. Fold in cranberries using just a few quick turn as berries will bleed out juice if over mixed with the batter.

Pour batter into a greased loaf pan. Bake for 45 to 55 minutes or until a toothpick inserted into the center comes out clean.

Applesauce Bread

1/2 C. vegetable oil
2 eggs
1 tsp. vanilla
1 C. applesauce
1/2 C. sour cream
1 tsp. cinnamon
2 1/2 C. Master Mix
1 C. oatmeal

Preheat oven to 350°.

In a large mixing bowl, mix the vegetable oil, eggs, vanilla, applesauce, sour cream and cinnamon until thoroughly combined.

Add Master Mix and oatmeal and stir until just combined.

Pour batter into a greased loaf pan. Bake for 55 to 65 minutes or until a toothpick inserted into the center comes out clean.

Raspberry
Milk Chocolate Bread

1/2 C. margarine, melted
2 eggs
1 C. milk
1 tsp. vanilla
3 C. Master Mix
1 1/2 C. chopped milk chocolate bars
1 C. raspberries (fresh or frozen,
    thawed)

Preheat oven to 350°.

In a large mixing bowl, mix the margarine, eggs, milk and vanilla until thoroughly combined.

Add Master Mix and stir until just combined. Fold in chocolate and raspberries using just a few quick turns as berries will bleed out juice if over mixed with the batter.

Pour batter into a greased loaf pan. Bake for 45 to 55 minutes or until a toothpick inserted into the center comes out clean.

Orange Banana Bread

1/2 C. vegetable oil
2 eggs
2 tsp. orange zest
1/2 C. orange juice
1/2 C. sour cream
1 C. mashed bananas (about 3 bananas)
3 C. Master Mix

82

Preheat oven to 350°.

In a large mixing bowl, mix the vegetable oil, eggs, orange zest, orange juice, sour cream and bananas until thoroughly combined.

Add Master Mix and stir until just combined.

Pour batter into a greased loaf pan. Bake for 55 to 65 minutes or until a toothpick inserted into the center comes out clean.

Holiday Loaf

1/2 C. margarine, melted
2 eggs
3/4 C. baking cocoa
1 tsp. mint extract
1 C. milk
2 1/2 C. Master Mix
1 C. mint chips
1 C. dried cherries

Preheat oven to 350°.

In a large mixing bowl, mix the margarine, eggs, cocoa, mint extract and milk until thoroughly combined.

Add Master Mix and stir until just combined. Fold mint chips and cherries into the batter.

Pour batter into a greased loaf pan. Bake for 45 to 55 minutes or until a toothpick inserted into the center comes out clean.

Peanut Butter & Banana Bread

1/3 C. margarine, melted
1/2 C. creamy peanut butter
2 eggs
1 tsp. vanilla
1 C. milk
1 C. mashed bananas (about 3 bananas)
3 C. Master Mix
3/4 C. chopped unsalted peanuts,
   optional

Preheat oven to 350°.

In a large mixing bowl, mix the margarine, peanut butter, eggs, vanilla, milk and bananas until thoroughly combined.

Add Master Mix and stir until just combined. Fold peanuts into the batter.

Pour batter into a greased loaf pan. Bake for 55 to 65 minutes or until a toothpick inserted into the center comes out clean.

Pear Loaf

1/2 C. margarine, melted
2 eggs
1/2 C. apple juice
1/2 C. milk
1/2 tsp. nutmeg
1 1/2 C. shredded fresh pears
3 C. Master Mix

Preheat oven to 350°.

In a large mixing bowl, mix the margarine, eggs, apple juice, milk, nutmeg and shredded pears until thoroughly combined.

Add Master Mix and stir until just combined.

Pour batter into a greased loaf pan. Bake for 55 to 65 minutes or until a toothpick inserted into the center comes out clean.

Craisin Bran Bread

1/2 C. vegetable oil
2 eggs
1/2 C. cranberry juice
1/2 C. milk
2 1/2 C. Master Mix
1 C. oat bran
1 C. craisins
3/4 C. chopped walnuts or pecans

Preheat oven to 350°.

In a large mixing bowl, mix the vegetable oil, eggs, cranberry juice and milk until thoroughly combined.

Add Master Mix and oat bran and stir until just combined. Fold craisins and walnuts or pecans into the batter.

Pour batter into a greased loaf pan. Bake for 45 to 55 minutes or until a toothpick inserted into the center comes out clean.

91

Sweet Cornmeal Bread

1/2 C. vegetable oil
2 eggs
1 C. milk
1 C. sweet corn (fresh or frozen,
    thawed)
2 1/4 C. Master Mix
1 C. yellow cornmeal

92

Preheat oven to 350°.

In a large mixing bowl, mix the vegetable oil, eggs, milk and sweet corn until thoroughly combined.

Add Master Mix and yellow cornmeal and stir until just combined.

Pour batter into a greased loaf pan. Bake for 45 to 55 minutes or until a toothpick inserted into the center comes out clean.

Chocolate Orange Bread

1/2 C. margarine, melted
2 eggs
3/4 C. baking cocoa
1 C. milk
1 C. mandarin oranges, coarsely chopped
2 tsp. orange zest
2 1/2 C. Master Mix

94

Preheat oven to 350°.

In a large mixing bowl, mix the margarine, eggs, cocoa, milk, mandarin oranges and orange zest until thoroughly combined.

Add Master Mix and stir until just combined.

Pour batter into a greased loaf pan. Bake for 45 to 55 minutes or until a toothpick inserted into the center comes out clean.

Banana Oat Bran Bread

1/2 C. vegetable oil
2 eggs
1 C. milk
1 tsp. vanilla
1/2 tsp. nutmeg
1 C. mashed bananas (about 3 bananas)
2 1/2 C. Master Mix
1 C. oat bran

96

Preheat oven to 350°.

In a large mixing bowl, mix the vegetable oil, eggs, milk, vanilla, nutmeg and bananas until thoroughly combined.

Add Master Mix and oat bran and stir until just combined.

Pour batter into a greased loaf pan. Bake for 55 to 65 minutes or until a toothpick inserted into the center comes out clean.

Blueberry Sour Cream Bread

1/2 C. margarine, melted
2 eggs
1 C. sour cream
1/3 C. milk
1/2 tsp. nutmeg
1 tsp. vanilla
3 C. Master Mix
3/4 C. chopped pecans or walnuts
1 C. blueberries (fresh or frozen, thawed)

Preheat oven to 350°.

In a large mixing bowl, mix the margarine, eggs, sour cream, milk, nutmeg and vanilla until thoroughly combined.

Add Master Mix and stir until just combined. Fold in pecans or walnuts and blueberries using just a few quick turns as berries will bleed out juice if over mixed with the batter.

Pour batter into a greased loaf pan. Bake for 55 to 65 minutes or until a toothpick inserted into the center comes out clean.

Strawberry & White Chocolate Bread

1 T. sugar
1 C. chopped strawberries (fresh or
    frozen, thawed)
1/2 C. margarine, melted
2 eggs
3/4 C. milk
1 tsp. vanilla
3 C. Master Mix
1 1/2 C. white chocolate chips

100

Preheat oven to 350°.

In a small bowl, sprinkle sugar over chopped strawberries. Mash coarsely with a fork, allowing the strawberries to bleed out juice.

In a large mixing bowl, mix the margarine, eggs, milk, strawberries with juice and vanilla until thoroughly combined.

Add Master Mix and stir until just combined. Fold white chocolate chips into the batter.

Pour batter into a greased loaf pan. Bake for 55 to 65 minutes or until a toothpick inserted into the center comes out clean.

Almond Citrus Bread

1/2 C. margarine, melted
2 eggs
3/4 C. sour cream
1/2 C. milk
1 tsp. orange extract
1 T. lemon zest
3 C. Master Mix
1 C. sliced almonds

Preheat oven to 350°.

In a large mixing bowl, mix the margarine, eggs, sour cream, milk, orange extract and lemon zest until thoroughly combined.

Add Master Mix and stir until just combined. Fold almonds into the batter.

Pour batter into a greased loaf pan. Bake for 45 to 55 minutes or until a toothpick inserted into the center comes out clean.

Hawaiian Loaf

1/2 C. vegetable oil
2 eggs
1-8 oz. can crushed pineapple
    including juice
1/2 C. milk
3 C. Master Mix
1 C. flaked or shredded coconut
3/4 C. chopped macadamia nuts

Preheat oven to 350°.

In a large mixing bowl, mix the vegetable oil, eggs, crushed pineapple and milk until thoroughly combined.

Add Master Mix and stir until just combined. Fold coconut and macadamia nuts into the batter.

Pour batter into a greased loaf pan. Bake for 45 to 55 minutes or until a toothpick inserted into the center comes out clean.

Index

108

Try all <u>4</u>
1 Master Mix books!